At the Zoo

Design and Art Direction
Lindaanne Donohoe Design

Illustrations
Penny Dann

● ● ● ● ● ● ● ● ● ● ● ● ● ● ●

Library of Congress Cataloging-in-Publication Data
Moses, Amy.
At the zoo/Amy Moses.
p.   cm.
Summary: Takes a trip through the zoo, pointing out some
of the animals, their physical characteristics, and habitats.
ISBN 1-56766-287-0 (hardcover)
1. Zoo animals—Miscellanea—Juvenile literature.
[1. Zoo animals 2. Animals. 3. Zoos.] I. Title.
QL77.5.M68   1997   96-5243
590'.74'4—DC20   CIP
                                                     AC

At the Zoo

By Amy Moses

Photographs by Phil Martin

The Child's World®

Zoos are home to living creatures from all over the world. What is your favorite wild animal?

The word zoo comes from the Greek word **zoe**. **Zoe** means life.

At the zoo, you can see many wild animals.
There are mammals, like elephants, and birds,
like toucans. There are reptiles, like snakes,
and amphibians, like alligators, who live
in water as well as on land.

Long ago, the first zoos belonged to kings and rulers. A private zoo was a sign of the ruler's wealth and power.

The ancient Greeks built zoos so people could learn about animals. Students visited these zoos. Today, students of all ages enjoy trips to zoos.

Chinese Emperor Wen Wang called his zoo "The Garden of Intelligence."

In the past, zoos kept animals in cages. Today, we know that animals are happier and healthier when they live like their wild cousins in open spaces.

Explorers came home with animals from other countries.

A designer builds an animal habitat with three things in mind. The first is the animal. "Will the animal be comfortable here?"

Animals need room to play.

**Next, designers think about zoo keepers:
"Will the keepers be able to care for the animals
easily and safely?"**

Meals for each animal are prepared in the zoo kitchen. They serve what the animals like to eat—from fruits and vegetables to insects.

Last, but not least, the designers think about the visitors. "Will the visitors get a good look at the animal?" Visitors enjoy seeing animals in their natural habitat.

Zoos have saved some species from extinction: the European bison, the Hawaiian goose, Père David's deer, and Przewalski's horse.

Animals are more active in a natural habitat exhibit than in a cage. Active animals are more likely to have babies. Many animals are born in zoos. Some are released into the wild when they are old enough to take care of themselves.

Did you know that the mother gorilla on page 18 is a hero? Her name is Binti-Jua, and she saved a little boy's life. After the boy fell into the ditch around her home, Binti ran over, picked him up, and carried him safely to a zookeeper.

Zoos once got all their animals from the wild. Today many animals are born and raised at the zoo. Zoos help to keep species from dying out. Are these kangaroos living in a zoo habitat or in the wild? Their zoo home is so well designed it is hard to tell.

Some animals are active at night. Their habitats have special lights so that visitors can see the animals when they are awake.

Who is at home in wide-open spaces?
Grazing animals, like giraffes, love grassland.
Hunting animals, like lions, need room to run.

Grazing animals eat plants. Hunting animals eat other animals.

Who likes the hot, steamy jungle?
Many different kinds of animals and plants
live here. This is a tropical rain forest.
Parrots, monkeys, pygmy hippos, and many
other animals love the jungle. There are
more kinds of animals in a rain forest than
anywhere else in the world.

Some of these plants are real and others are human-made.

Who lives in the ice and cold?
This weather is just right for puffins, penguins,
and polar bears. Animals that live in polar regions
wouldn't be happy in a warm climate.

Puffins can swim and fly. Penguins and polar bears are good swimmers.

Who is at home in the woodland forests?
Lemurs, monkeys, orangutans, and gorillas
live here. They need lots of trees to climb
and plenty of room to play.

Monkeys make up games.

Did you find your favorite animal here?
You can watch it all you want at the zoo.
A zoo is a place of wonder.

Glossary

amphibians—animals who live in water and on land

climate—weather; how hot or cold, wet or dry a place is

cousins—relations; descendants of a common ancestor

creatures—a name for living animals

designer—person who plans or thinks up new ways to build or make something

exhibit—a display built to show visitors a particular animal or thing

explorers—people who travel to new places looking for new lands or new information

extinction—the fact that a plant or animal will never again be found alive in nature

grassland—place where grass and other plants grow

habitat—the kind of place in nature where a plant or animal lives and grows strong

jungle—rain forest; a hot place where much rain falls and many plants and animals live

mammals—the kind of animals who have hair and are warm-blooded. Females give feed their milk from their bodies; humans and whales are mammals

natural—real; not made

polar regions—places in the far north and far south of the earth where it is always cold

pygmy—small-size

rain forest—another name for jungle

reptiles—cold blooded, usually egg-laying, animals covered with scales or horny plates

species—animals and plants that are of the same kind; human beings are a species

About the Author

Amy Moses writes books for children, teachers, and parents. She earned her masters degree in education with a Specialty in Reading. Amy is currently writing a novel. She loves reading, writing, making things, and being outdoors.